100 FACTS YOU SHOULD KNOW

OCEANS

By Clare Oliver

Gareth Stevens
PUBLISHING

Please visit our website, **www.garethstevens.com**. For a free color catalog of all our high-quality books, call toll free 1-800-542-2595 or fax 1-877-542-2596.

Oliver, Clare.
Oceans / by Clare Oliver.
p. cm. — (100 facts)
Includes index.
ISBN 978-1-4824-1305-2 (pbk.)
ISBN 978-1-4824-1263-5 (6-pack)
ISBN 978-1-4824-1465-3 (library binding)
1. Oceanography — Juvenile literature. 2. Ocean — Juvenile literature. 3. Marine ecology — Juvenile literature. I. Oliver, Clare. II. Title.
GC21.5 O45 2015
551.46—d23

Published in 2015 by
Gareth Stevens Publishing
111 East 14th Street, Suite 349
New York, NY 10003

Copyright © 2014 Miles Kelly Publishing Ltd

Publishing Director: Belinda Gallagher
Creative Director: Jo Cowan
Editorial Assistant: Amy Johnson
Volume Designer: Simon Lee

ACKNOWLEDGEMENTS
The publishers would like to thank the following artists who have contributed to this book:
Richard Burgess, Mike Foster
All other artworks from the Miles Kelly Artwork Bank

The publishers would like to thank the following sources for the use of their photographs:
Cover photograph: Cover (front) melissaf84/Shutterstock, (back, t) EpicStockMedia/Shutterstock, (cl) Leksele/Shutterstock, (cr) Mircea BEZERGHEANU/Shutterstock; Dreamstime 23(bl) Biolifepics; 30(m) Bluesunphoto; 42(c) Perstock; 43(cr) Bladerunner88; 45(cr) Expozer FLPA 24(t) Tui De Roy/Minden Pictures; 27(c) Norbert Wu/Minden Pictures   Fotolia 34(c) (paper) pdtnc   iStock 9(b) Joshua Haviv; 34(b) brytta   NPL 25(r) Jurgen Freund; 26(t) David; Shale; 28(m) Doug Perrine   Rex 38–39 W. Disney/Everett Shutterstock 1 and 21(t) Luna Vandoorne; 2–3 and 14(tr) agrosse; 5(tl) Richard Peterson, (tr) and 35(b) ANCH, (b) EpicStockMedia; 6–7(bg) Aubrey Laughlin, (m) ktsdesign; 11(t) fashcool, (b) Regien Paassen; 16–17(t) Boris Pamikov; 16(br) cynoclub; 17(b) Lynsey Allan; 19(b) Ian Scott; 20–21 powell'sPoint; 20(b) Eric Isselee; 22–23 Mariusz Potocki; 22(l) worldswildlifewonders; 23(t) Vladimir Melnik; 24(b) David Evison; 28(b) Arto Hakola; 29(m) foryouinf, (t) AridOcean; 30(b) Andrea Ricordi; 31(t) Gail Johnson, (bl) Jenny Leonard, (br) Mariko Yuki; 32–33 Rich Lindie; 32(t) steve estvanik; 33(br) BMJ; 34(t) DJTaylor; 35(t) Mark Hall; 36–37(bg) ilolab; 39(tr) Andrew Jalbert; 41(t) JonMilnes; 43(t) Dave Turner, (b) Ruth Peterkin; 44(m) Jeanne Provost, (b) CLChang; 45(t) Gustavo Miguel Fernandes, (b) Darren Brode
All other photographs are from: Corel, digitalSTOCK, digitalvision, iStockphoto.com, John Foxx, PhotoAlto, PhotoDisc, PhotoEssentials, PhotoPro, Stockbyte

Printed in the United States of America

CPSIA compliance information: Batch CS15GS: For further information contact Gareth Stevens, New York, New York at 1-800-542-2595.

Contents

Water world

1 Oceans cover more than two-thirds of the Earth's rocky surface. Their total area is about 140 million square miles (360 million sq km), which means there is more than twice as much ocean as land! Although all the oceans flow into each other, we know them as five different oceans – the Pacific, Atlantic, Indian, Southern, and Arctic. Our landmasses, the continents, rise out of the oceans.

ATLAN OCE

PACIFIC OCEAN

2 The largest, deepest ocean is the Pacific. It covers nearly half of our planet and is double the size of the Atlantic, the next largest ocean. In places, the Pacific is so deep that the Earth's tallest mountain, Everest, would sink without a trace.

▼ The point where the ocean meets the land is called the seashore.

3 Oceans can look blue, green, or gray. This is because of the way light hits the surface. Water soaks up the red parts of light but scatters the blue-green parts, making the sea look different shades of blue or green.

ARCTIC OCEAN

INDIAN OCEAN

SOUTHERN OCEAN

▲ Less than 10 percent of the world's oceans have been explored.

4 **Seas can be red or dead.** A sea is a small part of an ocean. The Red Sea, for example, is the part of the Indian Ocean between Egypt and Saudi Arabia. Asia's Dead Sea gets its name because it is so salty that most living things can't survive there.

5 **There are streams in the oceans.** All the water in the oceans is constantly moving, but in some places it flows as currents, which take particular paths. One of these is the warm Gulf Stream that travels around the edge of the Atlantic Ocean.

I DON'T BELIEVE IT!

Oceans hold 97 percent of the world's water. Just a fraction is in freshwater lakes and rivers.

Ocean features

6 There are plains, mountains, and valleys under the oceans in areas called basins. Each basin has a rim (the flat continental shelf that meets the shore) and sides (the continental slope that drops away from the shelf). In the ocean basin, there are flat abyssal plains, steep hills, huge underwater volcanoes called seamounts, and deep valleys called trenches.

Continental slope

Land

Continental shelf

Spreading ridge

Abyssal trench

Abyssal hills

▲ Under the oceans, there is a landscape similar to that found on land.

▼ As the magma (molten rock) cools, the ocean floor spreads out.

Spreading floor

Ridge

Magma

7 The ocean floor is spreading. Molten (liquid) rock inside the Earth seeps from holes on the seabed. As the rock cools, it forms new sections of floor that creep slowly out. Scientists have proved this fact by looking at layers of rock on the ocean floor. There are matching stripes of rock on either side of a ridge. Each pair came from the same hot-rock eruption, then slowly spread out.

Seamount

Volcanic island

Ocean trench

8 **Some islands are swallowed by the ocean.** Sometimes, a ring-shaped coral reef called an atoll marks where a volcanic island once was. The coral reef built up around the island. After the volcano sank underwater, the reef remained.

① Coral starts to grow

④ Coral atoll is left behind

② Lagoon appears around volcano

③ Volcano disappears

▲ An atoll is a ring-shaped coral reef that encloses a deep lagoon. It is left when an island sinks underwater.

9 **New islands are born all the time.** When an underwater volcano erupts, its lava cools in the water. Layers of lava build up, and the volcano grows in size. Eventually, it is tall enough to peep above the waves. The Hawaiian Islands rose from the sea like this.

I DON'T BELIEVE IT!

The world's longest mountain chain is under the ocean. It is the Mid-Ocean range and stretches around the middle of the Earth.

▶ The Hawaiian Islands were built up from layers of lava. There are still more to come.

Tides and shores

10 **The sea level rises and falls twice each day along the coast.** This is known as high and low tides. Tides happen because of the pull of the Moon's gravity, which lifts water from the part of the Earth's surface facing it.

▼ At high tide, the sea rises up the shore and dumps seaweed, shells, driftwood. Most coasts have two high tides and two low tides every d

High tides happen at the same time each day on opposite sides of the Earth

At high tide, the water level rises

At low tide, the water level goes down again

11 **Spring tides are especially high.** They occur twice a month, when the Moon is in line with the Earth and the Sun. Then, the Sun's pulling force joins the Moon's and seawater is lifted higher than usual. The opposite happens when the Moon and Sun are at right angles to each other. Then, their pulling powers work against each other causing weak neap tides – the lowest high tides and low tides.

► Spring tides occur when the Sun and the Moon are lined up and pulling together.

◄ Neap tides occur when the Sun and Moon are at right angles to each other and pulling in different directions.

12 The sea is strong enough to carve into rock. Pounding waves batter coastlines and erode, or wear away, the rock.

▼ Erosion can create amazing shapes such as arches and pillars called sea stacks.

Sea stack

Arch

13 Tsunamis are the most powerful waves. They happen when underwater earthquakes trigger tremendous shock waves. These whip up a wall of water that travels across the ocean's surface.

14 Sand is found on bars and spits, as well as beaches. It is made up of grains of worn-down rock and shell. Sand collects on shorelines and spits, but also forms on offshore beaches called sandbars. Spits are narrow ridges of worn sand and pebbles.

15 Some shores are swampy. This makes the border between land and sea hard to pinpoint. Muddy coastlines include tropical mangrove swamps that are flooded by salty water from the sea.

▶ The stilt roots of mangrove trees can take in nutrients from the water.

Life in a rock pool

16 Rock pools are teeming with all kinds of creatures. Limpets are a kind of shellfish. They live on rocks and in pools at shorelines. Here, they eat slimy, green algae, but they have to withstand the crashing tide. They cling to the rock with their muscular foot, only moving when the tide is out.

QUIZ

Can you find the names of four shells in the puzzle below?
1. alcm 2. lesmus
3. teroys 4. hewkl

Answers:
1. Clam 2. Mussel
3. Oyster 4. Whelk

17 Some anemones fight with harpoons. Beadlet anemones will sometimes fight over a feeding ground. Their weapon is the poison they usually use to stun their prey. They shoot tiny hooks like harpoons at each other until the weakest one gives in.

▶ Anemones are named after flowers, because of their petal-like arms.

▶ Starfish are relatives of brittle stars, sea urchins, and sea cucumbers.

18 Starfish can grow new arms. They may have as many as 40 arms, or rays. If a predator grabs hold of one, the starfish abandons the ray and uses the others to make its getaway!

19

Hermit crabs do not have shells. Most crabs shed their shells as they outgrow them, but the hermit crab does not have a shell. It borrows the leftover shell of a dead whelk or other mollusk, whatever it can squeeze into to protect its soft body. These crabs have even been spotted using a coconut shell as a home!

▶ Hermit crabs protect their soft bodies in a borrowed shell.

20

Sea urchins wear a disguise. Green sea urchins sometimes drape themselves with bits of shell, pebble, and seaweed. This makes the urchin more difficult for predators, or hunters, to spot.

21

Sponges are animals! They are very simple creatures that filter food from seawater. The natural sponge that you might use in the bath is a long-dead, dried-out sponge.

◀ There are about 4,500 different types of sponge in the sea.

Colorful coral

22 **Tiny animals build huge underwater walls.** These are built up from coral, the leftover skeletons of sea creatures called polyps. Over millions of years, enough skeletons pile up to form huge, wall-like structures called reefs. Coral reefs are full of hiding places and make great habitats for all sorts of amazing, colorful sea life.

▲ The Great Barrier Reef in Australia is the world's largest coral reef.

24 **The world's biggest shellfish lives on coral reefs.** Giant clams grow to well over 3 feet (1 m) long – big enough for you to bathe in its shell!

23 **Male seahorses have the babies.** They don't exactly give birth, but they store the eggs in a pouch on their belly. When the eggs are ready to hatch, a stream of miniature seahorses billows out from the male's pouch.

◄ Baby seahorses stream out of the male's pouch and into the sea.

Parrot fish

Giant clam

25 **Some fish go to the cleaners.** Cleaner wrasse are little fish that are paid for cleaning! Larger fish such as groupers and moray eels visit the wrasse, which eat all the parasites and other bits of dirt off the bigger fishes' bodies – what a feast!

26 **Clownfish are sting-proof.** Most creatures steer clear of an anemone's stinging tentacles. But the clownfish swims among the stingers, where it's safe from predators. Strangely, the anemone doesn't seem to sting the clownfish.

27 **Some fish look like stones.** Stone fish rest on the seabed, looking just like the rocks that surround them. If they are spotted, the poisonous spines on their backs can stun an attacker in seconds.

I DON'T BELIEVE IT!
You can see the Great Barrier Reef from space! At over 1,800 miles (2,900 km) long, it is the largest structure ever built by living creatures.

Lion fish

Cleaner wrasse fish

Stone fish

Clownfish

▲ Tropical coral reefs are the habitat of an amazing range of marine plants and creatures.

Swimming machines

28 There are over 21,000 different types of fish in the sea. They range from huge whale sharks to tiny gobies. Almost all are covered in scales and use fins and a muscular tail to power through the water. Like their freshwater cousins, sea fish have slits called gills that take oxygen from the water so they can breathe.

▶ In a large group called a school, fish like these yellow snappers have less chance of being picked off by a predator.

29 The oarfish is bigger than an oar — it can be as long as four canoes! It is the longest bony fish and is found in all the world's oceans. Oarfish are striking creatures — they have a red fin along the length of their back.

◀ People once thought oarfish swam horizontally through the water. Now we know they swim upright.

30 Sunfish like sunbathing! Ocean sunfish are very large, broad fish that can weigh up to one ton. They are named after their habit of sunbathing on the surface of the ocean.

◀ At over 10 feet (3 m) long, sunfish are the biggest bony fish in the oceans. They feed on plankton.

31 Flying fish cannot really fly. Fish can't survive out of water, but flying fish sometimes leap above the waves when they are travelling at high speeds. They use their wing-like fins to keep them in the air for as long as 30 seconds.

▲ Flying fish feed near the surface so they are easy to find. Their gliding flight helps them escape most hunters.

QUIZ

1. Which fish like to sunbathe?
2. How many types of fish live in the sea?
3. How does a fish breathe?
4. Can flying fish really fly?

Answers:
1. Sunfish 2. Over 21,000 3. With its gills 4. No

32 Not all fish are the same shape. Cod or mackerel are what we think of as a normal fish shape, but fish come in all shapes and sizes. Flounder and other flatfish have squashed-flat bodies. Eels are so long and thin that the biggest types look like snakes, while tiny garden eels resemble worms! And of course, seahorses and seadragons look nothing like other fish at all!

▶ The flounder's flattened shape and dull coloring help to camouflage (hide) it on the seabed.

Shark!

▼ Great white sharks are fierce hunters. They will attack and eat almost anything, but prefer to feed on seals.

33 **Great whites are the scariest sharks in the oceans.** These powerful predators have been known to kill people and can speed through the water at 35 miles (56 km) an hour. Unlike most fish, the great white is warm-blooded. This allows its muscles to work well, but also means the shark has to feed on plenty of meat.

▶ Basking sharks eat enormous amounts of plankton, which they sieve from the water as they swim.

34 **Most sharks are meat-eaters.** Herring are a favorite food for sand tiger and thresher sharks, while a tiger shark will eat just about anything! Strangely, some of the biggest sharks take the smallest prey. Whale sharks and basking sharks eat tiny sea creatures called plankton.

35 Sharks are shaped like torpedos. Most sharks are built for speed, with a long streamlined body. This means water can move past them easily. A shark's fins keep it the right way up in the water and help it to change direction quickly, so it can chase its prey. Sharks also have special cells in their heads, called ampullae of Lorenzini. These allow them to sense electricity given out by nearby fish.

I DON'T BELIEVE IT!

Some sharks, such as dogfish and zebra sharks, don't look after their pups. They leave them to fend for themselves.

Dorsal fin

Nostril

Jaw

Ampullae of Lorenzini

Gill

▶ The different features of a shark's body help it to be a successful hunter.

Pelvic fin

Anal fin

Pectoral fin

Tail fin

36 Hammerhead sharks have a hammer-shaped head! With a nostril and an eye on each end of the "hammer," they swing their head from side to side. This gives them double the chance to see and sniff out any signs of a tasty catch.

▲ Hammerheads prey on other sharks and rays, bony fish, crabs and lobsters, octopus, and squid.

Whales and dolphins

37 **The biggest animal on the planet lives in the oceans.** It is the blue whale, measuring about 100 feet (30 m) in length and weighing up to 200 tons (180 mt). It feeds by filtering tiny, shrimp-like creatures called krill from the water – about 4.5 tons (4 mt) of krill a day! Like other great whales, it has special, sieve-like parts in its mouth called baleen plates.

▶ The blue whale can be found in every ocean except the Arctic.

38 **Killer whales play with their food.** They especially like to catch baby seals, which they toss into the air before eating. Killer whales are not true whales, but the largest dolphins. They have teeth for chewing, instead of baleen plates.

▼ As the sperm whale surfaces, it pushes out stale air through its blowhole. It fills its lungs with fresh air and dives down again.

39 **Whales and dolphins have to come to the surface for air.** This is because they are mammals, like we are. Sperm whales hold their breath the longest. They have been known to stay underwater for nearly two hours.

40 Dolphins and whales sing songs to communicate. The noisiest is the humpback whale, whose wailing noises can be heard for hundreds of miles. The sweetest is the beluga – nicknamed the "sea canary." Songs are used to attract a mate, or just to keep track of each other.

▲ The beluga is a type of white whale. It makes a range of noises – whistles, clangs, chirps, and moos!

42 Moby-Dick was a famous fictional whale. It was featured in *Moby-Dick* (1851), a book by Herman Melville about a white sperm whale and a whaler called Captain Ahab.

41 The narwhal has a horn like a unicorn's. This Arctic whale has a long, twirly tooth that spirals out of its head. The males use their tusks as a weapon when they are fighting over females.

I DON'T BELIEVE IT!
Barnacles are shellfish. They attach themselves to ships' hulls, or the bodies of gray whales and other large sea animals.

▲ A male narwhal's tusk can grow to over 6.5 feet (2 m) long.

Sleek swimmers

43 **Whales and dolphins are not the only sea mammals.** Seals, sea lions, and walruses are warm-blooded mammals that have adapted to ocean life. These creatures are known as pinnipeds, meaning they have flippers instead of legs. They also have streamlined bodies and a layer of fatty blubber under the skin to keep them warm in chilly waters.

▼ Most seals live in cold waters. These crabeater seals live in Antarctica, as do leopard, Weddell, and fur seals. Northern seals, which live around the Arctic, include harp and bearded seals.

▼ Fights between male elephant seals during the breeding season can be extremely violent.

44 **Elephant seals are well-named – they are truly enormous!** Southern elephant seal males can weigh over 4 tons (3.6 mt), while their northern cousins weigh at least 2 tons (1.8 mt). During their three-month-long breeding season, males stay ashore to fight off rivals. Unable to hunt for fish, some lose as much as half their body weight.

45 **Walruses seem to change color!** When a walrus is in the water, it appears pale brown or even white. This is because blood drains from the skin's surface to stop the body losing heat. On land, the blood returns to the skin and walruses can look reddish brown or pink.

▼ Walruses use their tusks as weapons. They are also used to make breathing holes in the ice and to help the walrus pull itself out of the water.

46 **Sea otters anchor themselves when they sleep.** These playful creatures live off the Pacific coast among huge forests of giant seaweed called kelp. When they sleep, they wrap a strand of kelp around their body to stop them from being washed out to sea.

▼ Anchored to the kelp, a sea otter is free to rest.

Ocean reptiles

47 **Marine iguanas are the most seaworthy lizards.** Most lizards prefer life on land, where it is easier to warm up their cold-blooded bodies, but marine iguanas depend on the sea for food. They dive underwater to graze. When on land, the iguanas' dark skin absorbs the Sun's heat.

▼ Marine iguanas are found around the Galapagos Islands in the Pacific. They dive into the water to graze on seaweed and the algae growing on rocks.

▼ Female green turtles use their flippers to dig a large nest. Once they have laid their eggs, they cover the nest with sand.

48 **Turtles come ashore only to lay their eggs.** Although they are born on land, turtles head for the sea the minute they hatch. Females return to the beach where they were born to dig their nests. After they have laid their eggs, they go straight back to the water. Hawksbill turtles may lay up to 140 eggs in a clutch, while some green turtle females clock up 800 eggs in a year!

49 There are venomous (poisonous) snakes in the sea. Most stay close to land and come ashore to lay their eggs. Banded sea snakes, for example, cruise around coral reefs in search of their favorite food – eels. But the yellow-bellied sea snake never leaves the water. It gives birth to live babies in the open ocean.

▶ Banded sea snakes use venom (poison) to stun their prey.

▼ The yellow-bellied sea snake uses its colorful underside to attract fish. It then darts back – so the fish are next to its open mouth!

Yellow-bellied sea snake

Banded sea snake

50 Leatherback turtles dive up to 4,000 feet (1,219 m) for food. They hold the record for being the biggest sea turtles and for making the deepest dives. Leatherbacks feed mostly on jellyfish but their diet also includes mollusks, crabs, lobsters, and starfish.

▼ Leatherbacks are the biggest turtles in the world and can grow to 6.5 feet (2 m) in length.

Icy depths

51 Few creatures can survive in the dark, icy-cold ocean depths. Food is so hard to come by, the deep-sea anglerfish does not waste energy chasing prey. It has a stringy "fishing rod" with a glowing tip that extends from its dorsal fin or hangs above its jaw. This attracts smaller fish to the anglerfish's big mouth.

▲ Anglerfish are black or brown for camouflage. Only their glowing "fishing rod" is visible in the gloom.

Lantern fish

Cookie-cutter shark

Hatchet fish

52 Some deep-sea fish glow in the dark. As well as tempting prey, light also confuses predators. About 1,500 different deep-sea fish give off light. The lantern fish's whole body glows. The hatchet fish produces light along its belly and has silvery scales on its sides, which reflect light, confusing predators. Just the belly of the cookie-cutter shark gives off a ghostly glow.

◀ The light created by deep-sea fish, or by bacteria living on their bodies, is known as biological light, or bioluminescence.

53 **Black swallowers are greedy!** These strange fish are just 10 inches (25 cm) long but can eat fish far bigger than themselves. Their loose jaws unhinge to fit over the prey. Then the stretchy body expands to take in their enormous meal.

54 **Viperfish have teeth that are invisible in the dark.** They swim around with their jaws wide open. Deep-sea shrimp often see nothing until they are right inside the viperfish's mouth.

▶ The viperfish is named for its long, snake-like fangs.

55 **On the seabed, there are worms as long as cars!** These are giant tubeworms and they cluster around hot spots on the ocean floor. They feed on tiny particles that they filter from the water.

▲ The black swallower's stomach can stretch to take in prey twice its length.

▼ Bacteria inside the tubeworm turn minerals into food that the worm needs to survive.

Plume

Bacteria

Tube

Heart

Blood Vessel

I DON'T BELIEVE IT!
Female deep-sea anglerfish grow to 47 inches (120 cm) in length, but the males are a tiny 2.5 inches (6 cm)!

Amazing journeys

56 **Many ocean animals travel incredible distances.** Spiny lobsters spend the summer feeding off the coast of Florida, but head south in autumn to deeper waters. They travel about 30 miles (48 km) along the seabed, in columns that may be more than 50-strong. They keep together by touch, using their long, spiky antennae (feelers).

▼ In spring, spiny lobsters return to shallower waters. They spawn (lay their eggs) around the coral reefs off the Straits of Florida.

57 **Arctic terns are the long-distance flying champs.** These seabirds fly farther than any other bird. After nesting in the Arctic, they head south for the Antarctic. In its lifetime, one bird might cover more than 775,000 miles (1,247,000 km)!

▶ In a single year, an Arctic tern may fly more than 25,000 miles (40,230 km)!

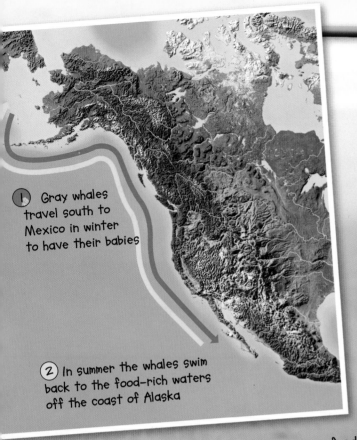

① Gray whales travel south to Mexico in winter to have their babies

② In summer the whales swim back to the food-rich waters off the coast of Alaska

58 Gray whales migrate, or travel, farther than any other mammal. There are two main gray whale populations in the Pacific. One spends summer off the Alaskan coast. In winter they migrate south to Mexico to breed. The whales may swim nearly 12,500 miles (20,100 km) in a year. The other gray whale group spends summer off the coast of Russia, then travels south to Korea.

▲ Gray whales spend the summer in the Bering Sea, feeding on tiny, shrimp–like creatures called amphipods. They spend their breeding season, December to March, in warmer waters.

I DON'T BELIEVE IT!
Eels and salmon swim thousands of miles from the sea to spawn in the same river nurseries where they were born.

▲ As soon as they are born, loggerhead hatchlings crawl down to the water, to avoid being picked off by hungry gulls or crabs.

59 Baby loggerhead turtles make a two–year journey. They are born on beaches in Japan. The hatchlings hurry down to the sea and set off across the Pacific to Mexico, a journey of 6,000 miles (9,700 km). They spend about five years there before returning to Japan to breed.

On the wing

QUIZ

1. How long is the wingspan of an albatross?
2. Where do puffins dig their burrows?
3. How do gannets dive for fish?
4. What color is a male frigate bird's pouch?

Answers:
1. Up to 11 feet (3.4 m) 2. On clifftops 3. Headfirst into the ocean 4. Bright red

60 **Wandering albatrosses are the biggest seabirds.** An albatross has a wingspan of around up to 11 feet (3.4 m) – about the length of a family car! These seabirds are so large, they take off by launching from a cliff. Albatrosses spend months at sea. To feed, they land on the sea, where they sit and catch creatures such as squid.

▶ Albatrosses are such expert gliders that they can even sleep while flying.

▼ Puffins often scrape their own burrows on clifftops, or they may take over an abandoned rabbit hole.

61 **Puffins nest in burrows.** While many birds jostle for space on a high cliff ledge, puffins dig a burrow on the clifftop. Here, they lay a single egg. Both parents feed the chick for the first six weeks.

62 **Gannets wear air-bag shock absorbers.** The gannet's feeding technique is to plummet headfirst into the ocean and catch a fish in its beak. It dives at high-speed and hits the water hard. Luckily, the gannet's head is protected with sacs of air that absorb most of the shock.

▲ When a gannet spots its meal, it dives into the water at high speed to catch it.

63 **Frigate birds puff up a balloon for their mate.** Male frigate birds have a bright-red pouch on their throat. They inflate, or blow up, the pouch as part of their display to attract a female.

► A blue-footed booby displays its blue feet.

▼ A frigate bird shows off to its mate.

64 **Boobies dance to attract a mate.** There are two types of booby, blue- or red-footed. The dancing draws attention to the male's colorful feet. Perhaps this stops the females from mating with the wrong type of bird.

Perfect penguins

65 Macaroni, Chinstrap, and Emperor are all types of penguin. There are 17 different types in total, and most live around the Antarctic. Penguins feed on fish, squid, and krill. Their black-and-white plumage is important camouflage. Seen from above, a penguin's black back blends in with the water. The white belly is hard to distinguish from the sunlit surface of the sea.

▼ King penguins live near Antarctica. Like all penguins, they have a layer of fat under their feathers to protect them in the icy water.

66 Penguins can swim, but not fly. They have oily, waterproofed feathers and flipper-like wings. Instead of lightweight, hollow bones – like a flying bird's – some penguins have solid, heavy bones. This enables them to stay underwater longer when diving for food. Emperor penguins c[a] stay under for 15 minutes or more.

67 Some penguins build stone circles. This is the way that Adélie and Gentoo penguins build nests on the shingled shores where they breed. First, they scrape out a small dip with their flippered feet and then they surround the hollow with a circle of pebbles.

▲ An Adélie penguin builds i[ts nest] from stones and small rocks.

▼ The different types of penguin vary in shape, size, and appearance.

Rockhopper   Macaroni   Royal   Chinstrap   Gentoo

68 **Emperor penguin dads balance an egg on their feet.** They do this to keep their egg off the Antarctic ice, where it would freeze. The female leaves her mate with the egg for the whole two months that it takes to hatch. The male has to go without food during this time. When the chick hatches, the mother returns and both parents help to raise it.

▶ A downy Emperor penguin chick cannot find its own food in the sea until it has grown its waterproof adult plumage. In the meantime, its parents feed and care for it.

Harvests from the sea

69 **Oysters come from beds – and lobsters from pots!** The animals in the oceans feed other sea creatures, and they feed us, too! To gather oysters, fishermen raise them on trays or poles in the water. First, they collect oyster larvae, or babies. They attract them by putting out sticks hung with shells. Lobster larvae are too difficult to collect, but the adults are caught in pots filled with fish bait.

▲ Bait is placed in lobster pots like these. Once a lobster has entered, it can't escape.

70 **Some farmers grow seaweed.** Seaweed is delicious to eat and is also a useful ingredient in products such as ice cream and plant fertilizer. In shallow, tropical waters, people grow their own on plots of seabed.

▼ A woman harvests seaweed on a farm on the coast of Zanzibar, East Africa.

71

Sea minerals are big business. Minerals are useful substances that we mine from the ground – and oceans are full of them! The most valuable are oil and gas, which are pumped from the seabed and piped ashore or transported in huge supertankers. Salt is another important mineral. In hot, low-lying areas, people build walls to hold shallow pools of sea water. The water dries up in the sun, leaving behind crystals of salt.

72

There are gemstones under the sea. Pearls are made by oysters. If a grain of sand is lodged inside an oyster's shell, it irritates its soft body. The oyster coats the sand with a substance called nacre, which is also used to line the inside of the shell. Over the years, more nacre builds up and the pearl gets bigger.

▲ The oil platform's welded-steel legs rest on the seabed. They support the platform around 50 feet (15 m) above the surface of the water.

▶ An oyster's shell must be pried open with a knife to get to the pearl inside.

QUIZ

1. What are the young of lobster called?
2. What substances are pumped from the seabed?
3. Is seaweed edible?
4. Which gemstone is made by oysters?

Answers:
1. Larvae 2. Oil and gas
3. Yes 4. Pearl

33

First voyages

73 **The first boats were made from tree trunks.** Early people hollowed out tree trunks to craft their own dug-outs. For several hundred years, the Maori peoples of New Zealand made log war canoes, decorating them with beautiful carvings.

▼ Maori war canoes were usually carved out of kauri pine trunks.

74 **Greek warships were oar-some!** The ancient Greeks used people-power and sails to move their ships through the water. Triremes were warships rowed by three layers of oarsmen. In battle, the trireme was steered straight at an enemy ship like a battering ram.

▶ A painted eye on the trireme's hull was believed to protect the boat from evil spirits.

▼ Viking longboats were clinker-built, which means that they were made of overlapping planks of wood.

77 **Boats were used to find the way to a new world.** The 1400s were an amazing time of exploration and discovery. One explorer, Christopher Columbus, set sail from Spain in 1492 with a fleet of three ships. He hoped to find a new trade route to India, but instead he found the Americas. Before then, they were not even on the map!

75 **Dragons guarded Viking longboats.** Scandinavian seafarers decorated their boats' prows with carvings of dragons and serpents to terrify their enemies. Built from overlapping planks, Viking longboats were very seaworthy. Leif Eriksson was the first Viking to cross the Atlantic Ocean to Newfoundland, in North America, just over 1,000 years ago.

▼ Columbus's fleet consisted of the *Niña*, the *Pinta*, and the *Santa Maria*.

76 **It is** thought that Chinese navigators made the first compass-like device about 2,500 years ago. Compasses use the Earth's magnetism to show the directions of north, south, east, and west. They are used at sea, where there are no landmarks. The navigators used lodestone, a naturally magnetic rock, to magnetize the needle.

▶ Early compasses were very simple. During the 1300s compasses became more detailed.

QUIZ

Unscramble the letters to find the names of six different types of boat.
1. leacvar 2. chenroos
3. rarlewt 4. coclear
5. leglay 6. pecpril

Answers:
1. Caravel 2. Schooner
3. Trawler 4. Coracle
5. Galley 6. Clipper

Pirates!

78 **The high seas were once ruled by pirates.** Pirates are sailors who attack other ships to steal their cargoes. Their golden age was the 1600s and 1700s. This was when heavily laden ships carried treasures, weapons, and goods back to Europe from colonies in the Americas, Africa, and Asia. Edward Teach, better known as Blackbeard, was one of the most terrifying pirates. He attacked ships off the coast of North America during the early 1700s.

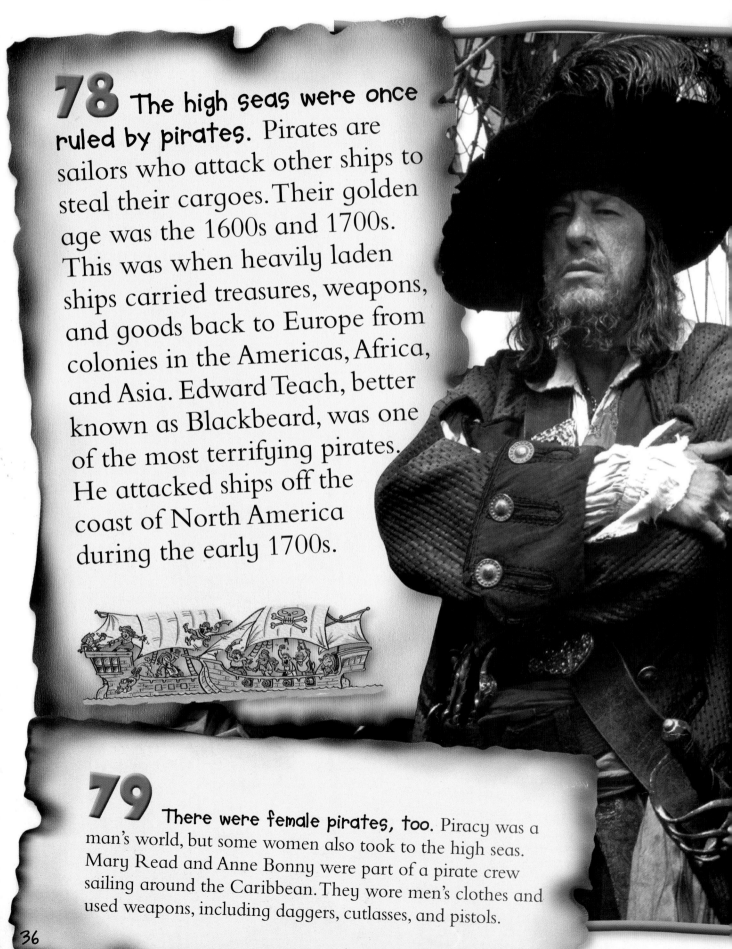

79 **There were female pirates, too.** Piracy was a man's world, but some women also took to the high seas. Mary Read and Anne Bonny were part of a pirate crew sailing around the Caribbean. They wore men's clothes and used weapons, including daggers, cutlasses, and pistols.

80 **There are still pirates on the oceans.** Despite police patrols that watch for pirates and smugglers, a few pirates still operate. Luxury yachts are an easy target, and in the South China Sea, pirate gangs on motorboats even attack large merchant ships.

► Divers have found some extraordinary hoards of treasure on board sunken galleons.

▼ *Pirates of the Caribbean: The Curse of the Black Pearl* (2003) told the story of a group of pirates cursed for stealing treasure.

81 **There is treasure lying under the sea.** Over the centuries, many ships have sunk in storms or hit reefs. They include pirate ships loaded with stolen booty. Some ships were deliberately sunk by pirates. The bed of the Caribbean Sea is littered with the remains of Spanish galleons, many of which still hold treasure!

MAKE A PIRATE FLAG!

You will need:
paper   paints   brushes

The skull-and-crossbones is the most famous pirate flag, but it was not the only one. Copy one of these designs!

37

Going under

82 A submarine has dived deeper than 35,000 feet (10,670 m). The two-person *Trieste* made history in 1960 in an expedition to the Mariana Trench in the Pacific, the deepest part of any ocean. It took the submarine five hours to reach the bottom, a distance of 35,800 feet (10,911 m). On the way down, the extreme water pressure cracked part of the craft, but luckily, the two men inside returned to the surface unharmed.

▲ *Trieste* spent 20 minutes at the bottom of the Mariana Trench.

Mast to renew and expel air

Propellers

Mine

◄ The Americans used *Turtle* against the British in the Revoluntionary War.

83 The first combat submarine was shaped like an egg! *Turtle* was a one-person submarine that made its test dive in 1776. It was the first real submarine. It did not have an engine – it was driven by a propeller turned by hand. *Turtle* was built for war. It travelled just below the surface and could fix bombs to the bottom of enemy ships.

84 **Divers have a spare pair of lungs.** Scuba divers wear special breathing apparatus called "aqua lungs." French divers Jacques Cousteau and Emile Gagnan came up with the idea of a portable oxygen supply. This meant that divers were able to swim freely for the first time, rather than wearing a heavy suit and helmet.

▲ Divers control their breathing to make their oxygen supply last as long as possible.

85 **The biggest submarines weighed 29,200 tons (26,500 mt).** They were Russian submarines called Typhoons, built in the 1970s and 1980s. As well as being the biggest submarines, they were also the fastest, able to top 40 knots.

Periscope

Rudder

▼ The Typhoons did not need to come up to refuel because they were nuclear-powered.

Engine room

Living quarters

Torpedo firing tube

I DON'T BELIEVE IT!

In 1963 Jacques Cousteau built a village on the bed of the Red Sea. Along with four other divers, he lived there for a whole month.

Diving plane

Superboats

86
Some ships are invisible. Stealth warships are not really invisible, of course, but they are hard to detect using radar. There are already materials being used for ships that can absorb some radar signals. Some paints can soak up radar, too, and signals are also bounced off in confusing directions by the ships' strange, angled hulls.

▶ An angled, sloping hull gives very little radar echo. This makes the stealth ship's location hard to pinpoint.

87
The biggest ship ever built was nearly a third of a mile (0.5 km) long. It was a supertanker called *Jahre Viking*. Supertankers carry cargoes of oil around the world. They move slowly because they are so huge and heavy. *Jahre Viking* was demolished in 2009. The world's biggest ship is now a container ship called *CMA CGM Marco Polo*.

▼ The giant supertanker *Jahre Viking* was just over 1,500 feet (457 m) long.

▼ Hovercraft can travel at up to 65 knots, the equivalent of 75 miles (120 km) an hour.

88 **Not all boats ride the waves.** Hovercrafts sit slightly above the water. They have a rubbery "skirt" that traps a cushion of air for them to ride on. Without the drag of the water to work against, hovercraft can cross the water much faster.

89 **Ships can give piggybacks!** Heavy-lift ships can sink part of their deck underwater, so a smaller ship can sail aboard for a free ride. Some ships carry planes. Aircraft carriers transport planes that are too small to carry enough fuel for long distances. The deck doubles up as a runway, where the planes take off and land.

▼ Some cruise ships stop at different ports during the journey, while others only stop at the beginning and end.

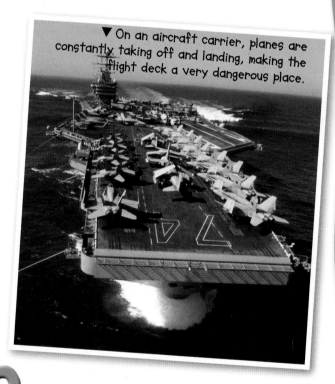

▼ On an aircraft carrier, planes are constantly taking off and landing, making the flight deck a very dangerous place.

90 **Cruise ships are floating holidays.** They are among the largest ships on the oceans today. Cruise ships usually have lots of different features, such as restaurants, shops, swimming pools, casinos, spas, and bowling alleys. The biggest cruise ship in the world is currently *Allure of the Seas*, at over 1,180 feet (360 m) in length.

Riding the waves

91 **The first sea sport was surfing.** It took off in the 1950s, but was invented centuries earlier in Hawaii. Hawaii is still one of the best places to surf – at Waimea Bay, surfers catch waves that are up to 36 feet (11 m) high. The record for the longest rides, though, are made off the coast of Mexico, where it is possible to surf for more than 1 mile (1.6 km).

▼ Modern surfboards are made of super-light materials. This means they create little drag in the water – and the surfer can reach high speeds!

92 **A single boat towed 100 water-skiers!** This record was made off the coast of Australia in 1986, and no one has beaten it yet. The drag boat was a cruiser called *Reef Cat*.

▶ Water-skiing is now one of the most popular of all water sports.

QUIZ

1. What was the name of the fastest hydroplane?
2. When were Jet-Skis developed?
3. Where is Waimea Bay?
4. What is a trimaran?

Answers:
1. *Spirit of Australia*
2. 1960s 3. Hawaii
4. A three-hulled boat

94 **Three hulls are sometimes better than one.** Powerboating is an exciting, dangerous sport. Competitors are always trying out new boat designs that will race even faster. Multi-hulled boats minimize drag, but keep the boat steady. Trimarans have three slender, streamlined hulls that cut through the water.

93 **Jet-Skiers can travel at nearly 62 miles (100 km) an hour.** Jet Skis were first developed in the 1960s. Their inventor was an American called Clayton Jacobsen who wanted to combine his two favorite hobbies, motorbikes and water-skiing. Today, some Jet-Skiers are professional athletes.

▶ Trimarans have three hulls, while catamarans have two.

95 **Hydroplanes fly over the waves.** They are a cross between a boat and a plane. Special "wings" raise the hull 6.5 feet (2 m) above the water. The fastest hydroplane ever was *Spirit of Australia*. Driven by Kenneth Warby, it sped along at more than 310 miles (500 km) an hour above the surface of the water!

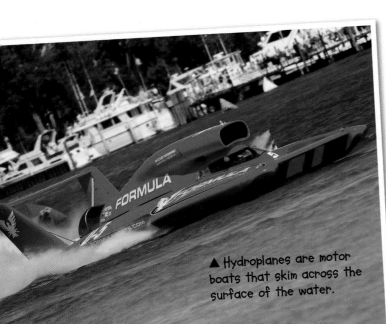

▲ Hydroplanes are motor boats that skim across the surface of the water.

Ocean stories

96 **The Greek hero Jason made an epic sea voyage.** The ancient Greeks made up lots of sea adventure stories, probably because they lived on scattered islands. In the legend of the Argonauts, a hero called Jason sets off in a boat called the *Argo* with a band of brave men. He goes on a quest to find the Golden Fleece, a precious sheepskin guarded by a fierce dragon.

▲ Jason and the Argonauts steer their ship between two huge moving cliffs called the Cyanean Rocks. They faced many dangers on their journey.

▼ Neptune raises his trident and whips up a storm.

97 **Neptune (or Poseidon) was an undersea god.** Poseidon was the name used by the ancient Greeks and Neptune by the ancient Romans. Both civilizations pictured their god with a fork called a trident. They blamed their gods for the terrible storms that wrecked boats in the Mediterranean.

eautiful goddess Aphrodite
from the sea.

99
Long ago, people believed in a giant sea monster called the **kraken.** The stories were used to explain the dangers of the sea. Sightings of the giant squid might have inspired these tales.

▶ Mistaken for a monster! The 50-foot (15 m) long giant squid has eyes as big as dinner plates.

98
The Greek goddess of love was born in the sea. Aphrodite was said to be the daughter of Zeus, the king of the gods. She was born out of the foam of the sea. The Romans based their love goddess, Venus, on the same story. Lots of artists have painted her rising from the waves in a giant clam shell.

100
Mermaids lured sailors to their deaths on the rocks. Mythical mermaids were said to be half-woman, half-fish. Folklore tells how the mermaids confused sailors with their beautiful singing – with the result that their ships were wrecked on the rocks.

▼ Mermaids were said to have the tail of a fish instead of legs.

I DON'T BELIEVE IT!
A mermaid's purse is the name given to the eggcases of the dog shark. They look a little bit like handbags!

Glossary

abyssal: relating to the bottom waters of the oceans

demolish: to destroy or forcefully tear apart

distinguish: to notice something or recognize a difference between things. Also, to make something different from something else.

dorsal: relating to or placed near or on the back of an animal

erupt: to send out rocks, ash, or lava in a sudden explosion

fertilizer: a substance that is added to soil to help the growth of plants

hull: the main part of a ship or boat

irritate: to make part of the body sore or painful

laden: to put a load or burden on or in

mangrove: a tropical tree that has roots which grow from its branches and that grows in shallow salt water

navigator: a person who finds out how to get to a place

nuclear: relating to, producing, or using energy that is created when the nuclei of atoms are split apart or joined together

sieve: a tool that has many small holes and that is used to separate smaller particles from larger ones or solids from liquids

technique: a way of doing something using special knowledge or skills

tentacle: one of the long, flexible arms of an animal that are used for grabbing things and moving

For More Information

Books

Callery, Sean, and David Burnie. *Ocean*. New York, NY: Kingfisher, 2011.

Franklin, Carolyn. *Ocean Life*. New York, NY: Children's Press, 2008.

Gordon, Sharon. *Ocean Animals*. New York, NY: Marshall Cavendish Benchmark, 2009.

Hoffman, Jennifer. *Ocean Science*. New York, NY: Collins, 2007.

Woodward, John. *Oceans*. New York, NY: DK Publishing, 2008.

Websites

Marine Life
marinebio.org/oceans/creatures.asp
Check out cool videos and awesome facts about ocean life.

The Ocean
ocean.nationalgeographic.com/ocean/
See amazing photographs and read interesting information about oceans and marine life.

Scholastic Explorers: Ocean Life
teacher.scholastic.com/activities/explorer/oceanlife/
Learn how people explore the inner depths of the ocean.

Index